Piano Sketches

Duets

Vitalij Neugasimov

Book 1

6 easy pieces for piano four-hands

T0057072

MUSIC DEPARTMENT

OXFORD
UNIVERSITY PRESS

OXFORD
UNIVERSITY PRESS

Great Clarendon Street, Oxford OX2 6DP,
United Kingdom

Oxford University Press is a department of the University of Oxford.
It furthers the University's objective of excellence in research, scholarship,
and education by publishing worldwide. Oxford is a registered trade mark of
Oxford University Press in the UK and in certain other countries

This collection © Oxford University Press 2017

Vitalij Neugasimov has asserted his right under the Copyright, Designs
and Patents Act, 1988, to be identified as the Composer of these Works

Database right Oxford University Press (maker)

First published 2017

Impression: 1

All rights reserved. No part of this publication may be reproduced,
stored in a retrieval system, or transmitted, in any form or by any means,
without the prior permission in writing of Oxford University Press

Permission to perform this work in public (except in the course of divine worship) should
normally be obtained from the Performing Right Society Ltd (PRS) at www.prsformusic.com
or a local performing right licensing organization, unless the owner or the occupier
of the premises being used already holds a licence from such an organization.
Likewise, permission to make and exploit a recording must be obtained in advance from
the Mechanical-Copyright Protection Society Ltd (MCPS) at www.prsformusic.com or
a local mechanical copyright licensing organization

Enquiries concerning reproduction outside the scope of the above
should be directed to the Music Rights Department, Oxford University Press, at
music.permissions.uk@oup.com or at the address above

ISBN 978-0-19-351765-3

Music and text origination by Katie Johnston

Printed in Great Britain on acid-free paper by
Halstan & Co. Ltd, Amersham, Bucks.

Thank you so much to my sister Liudmila Neugasimova, an exceptional piano teacher, for her invaluable contribution, brilliant ideas, encouragement, and support.

Contents

	Level (approx. ABRSM grade)		Page
	Primo	Secondo	
Raindrops in the Morning	2	3	4
Wind of Spring	2	3	8
Just for You	3	2	12
High in the Sky	3	3	18
Crazy Clown	3	3	22
The Glorious Pastime	3	3	28

Performance, backing and practice tracks are available on the Companion Website: www.oup.com/pianosketchesduets.

Durations are given below each piece.

Raindrops in the Morning

© Oxford University Press 2017. Photocopying this copyright material is ILLEGAL.

Raindrops in the Morning

Vitalij Neugasimov

Duration: c.2 mins

© Oxford University Press 2017. Photocopying this copyright material is ILLEGAL.

22
p
26
legato e più espressivo
cresc.
con Ped.
30
34
f
senza Ped.
38
mf
42
mp
p
pp
con Ped.

22
mp
26
legato e più espressivo
cresc.
30
34
f
38
mf
42
mp
p
pp

Wind of Spring

Vitalij Neugasimov

© Oxford University Press 2017. Photocopying this copyright material is ILLEGAL.

Wind of Spring

Vitalij Neugasimov

Duration: c.1.5 mins

© Oxford University Press 2017. Photocopying this copyright material is ILLEGAL.

25
30
poco rit.
cresc.
35
a tempo
mf
39
43
mp
47
rit.

25
30
poco rit.
cresc.
a tempo
35
8va
f
39
(8va)
43
(8va)
mf
47
(8va)
rit.

Just for You

Vitalij Neugasimov

© Oxford University Press 2017. Photocopying this copyright material is ILLEGAL.

Just for You

Vitalij Neugasimov

Duration: *c.*3 mins

© Oxford University Press 2017. Photocopying this copyright material is ILLEGAL.

17
21
25
non legato
29
p
33

17
21
mp semplice
25
8va
29
mf più espressivo
sim.
33
(8va)
cresc.
dim.

37
41
mp
45
49
meno mosso ♩ = 69
pp
53
rall.
Ped.

37
(8va)
2
più f
mf
41
meno f
mf
45
mp
49
meno mosso ♩ = 69
pp
53
rall.

High in the Sky

Vitalij Neugasimov

© Oxford University Press 2010 and 2017. Photocopying this copyright material is ILLEGAL.

High in the Sky

Vitalij Neugasimov

Duration: c.1.5 mins

© Oxford University Press 2010 and 2017. Photocopying this copyright material is ILLEGAL.

15
sub. p
pp
5
18
cresc.
1
21
mf
mp
2
5-3
24
cresc.
f
rall.
27
1 4
2
poco a poco dim.
1-5

15
sub. p
pp
18
cresc.
21
mf
mp
24
cresc.
f
27
rall.
poco a poco dim.

Crazy Clown

Vitalij Neugasimov

© Oxford University Press 2017. Photocopying this copyright material is ILLEGAL.

Crazy Clown

Vitalij Neugasimov

Duration: c.1.5 mins

© Oxford University Press 2017. Photocopying this copyright material is ILLEGAL.

25
30
mf
p
36
sub. f
41
p
cresc.
47
mf
sim.

25
30
f
mp
36
sub. f
41
mp dolce e con passione
cresc.
47
f

52
sub. p
57
mf
63
sim.
69
meno f
75
f

52
sub. mp
57
63
f
69
meno f
75
ff

The Glorious Pastime

Vitalij Neugasimov

© Oxford University Press 2017. Photocopying this copyright material is ILLEGAL.

The Glorious Pastime

Vitalij Neugasimov

Duration: c.2 mins

© Oxford University Press 2017. Photocopying this copyright material is ILLEGAL.

17
mf
21
meno mosso ♩ = 66
p
25
29
Tempo primo
mf
32
mp
35
rit.
mf

17
mf
21
meno mosso ♩ = 66
p
25
29
Tempo primo
mf
32
mp
35
rit.
mf